All Aboard with Bulletin Boards

by

Robyn Spizman

illustrated by Evelyn Pesiri

Cover by Dan Grossman

Copyright © Good Apple, Inc., 1983

ISBN No. 0-86653-105-X

Printing No. 9876

GOOD APPLE, INC.
BOX 299
CARTHAGE, IL 62321-0299

TABLE OF CONTENTS

INTRODUCTION

Dear Teachers:

This book was designed to give you 180 bulletin boards on all subject areas carefully developed to stimulate your students and brighten your classroom. Consider it a valuable resource for years to come. A special word of thanks goes to my ingenious artist Evelyn Pesiri. Her magical touch added the necessary ingredients to make this book a success.

HOW TO USE THIS BOOK

This book offers you illustrated bulletin boards on almost every subject imaginable. Each identifies its own purpose and proceeds to give helpful tips when necessary. For enlarging characters, an overhead or opaque projector can be used, or try drawing and enlarging characters freehand.

LETTERING

For successful lettering, try making your own sets from precut stencils. Cutting your own letters is also fun, but it takes patience and practice.

BORDERS

Borders help put the finishing touch on a bulletin board. They can be made from a variety of materials, from corrugated paper to construction paper.

BACKGROUND MATERIALS

The choice of a background material is very important to the overall success of your bulletin board. Choose one that will work with your total scheme. There are many excellent choices, but I found mural paper (available in a variety of colors) was always a great choice. Another wonderful background is burlap. Carefully hang it and when it fades, simply reverse it and use the other side.

IN CONCLUSION

Take advantage of your most valuable resource---your students. Involve your class in creating your bulletin boards. Also create an idea file with your bulletin board ideas. Take the time when changing boards to identify and file each set of letters and accompanying illustrations. This proves to be an excellent time-saver.
I sincerely hope this book will be the helpful resource it is intended to be.
...And once again....here's to you—the future of our creative and enlightened classrooms.
PLAN....PREPARE...AND PROUDLY PRESENT!

Best wishes,

ALPHABET

Purpose: This bulletin board will encourage students to study and master the alphabet.

Purpose: Use this bulletin board to excite students about learning the alphabet.

ALPHABET

ABCDEFGHIJKLMNOPQRSTUVWXYZ

ATTENTION Please!

FOR THE ABC'S

Purpose: This bulletin board will announce the wonderful world of the alphabet. Hide letters in your classroom and have an alphabet hunt.

AHOY MATES, THE ALPHABET'S GREAT

Purpose: Use this bulletin board to reinforce students' skills in alphabetizing.

ART

Purpose: Use this bulletin board to stimulate students to be interested in art. Display this board when introducing primary and secondary colors.

Purpose: Use this bulletin board to call attention to student artwork.

ART

Purpose: Use this bulletin board to illustrate the variety of materials used in art. Have a multimedia art lesson!

. . . .

Purpose: Use this bulletin board to display student artwork.

ART

Purpose: Use this bulletin board to express the universal appreciation of art. Introduce art from different cultures.

Purpose: Use this bulletin board in October to display student artwork. Have students create Halloween paintings.

ART

TREASURES AWAIT YOU IN ART

Purpose: Use this bulletin board to encourage students to be excited about art. Have students paint pictures of things they treasure.

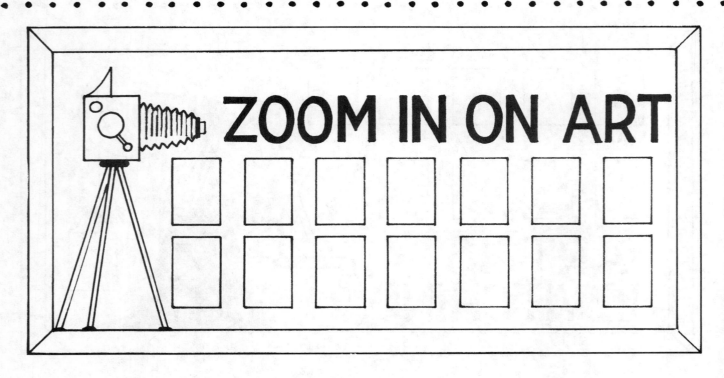

ZOOM IN ON ART

Purpose: Use this bulletin board to introduce the art of photography and for displaying student work.

6

Purpose: Use this bulletin board to encourage students to pursue a career. Have students interview people about their careers.

Purpose: Use this bulletin board to motivate students to explore a variety of careers.

Purpose: Use this bulletin board to encourage students to be aware of a variety of careers.

Purpose: Use this bulletin board to increase students' knowledge of the want ads and a variety of careers.

CAREER AWARENESS

GET IN GEAR WITH A CAREER

Purpose: Use this bulletin board to promote career awareness.

GET A KICK OUT OF CAREERS

Purpose: Use this bulletin board to promote career awareness.

9

STEER A CAREER ON COURSE

Purpose: Use this bulletin board to encourage career awareness. Create a list of classroom jobs and let students apply for them.

THREE CHEERS FOR *Careers*

Purpose: Use this bulletin board to stimulate an interest in career awareness.

LET THE DICTIONARY DAZZLE YOU!

DICTIONARY

Purpose: Use this bulletin board to increase students' use of a dictionary. Add words that you want the students to define to the dictionary.

DICTIONARIES ARE DELICIOUS

DICTIONARY

Purpose: This bulletin board will motivate students to use the dictionary.

Purpose: This bulletin board will encourage students to use a dictionary.

Purpose: Use this bulletin board to encourage students to use a dictionary.

DICTIONARY

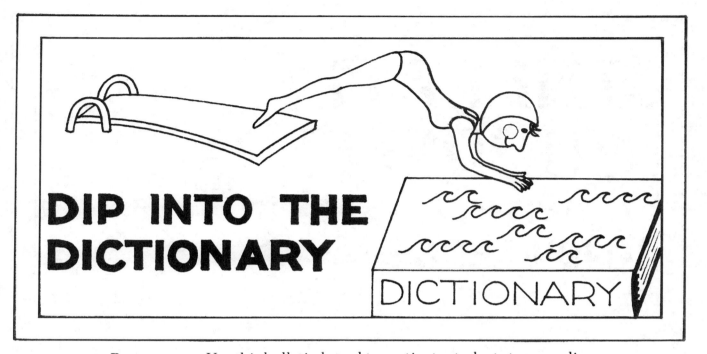

Purpose: Use this bulletin board to motivate students to use a dictionary.

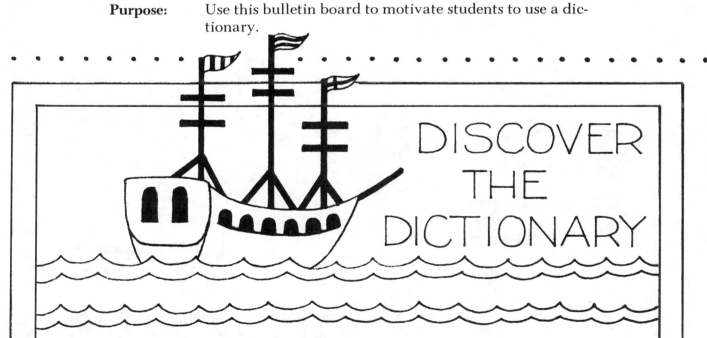

Purpose: Use this bulletin board to excite students about using the dictionary.

EDUCATION

Purpose: This bulletin board will stress the importance of education and learning.

Purpose: Use this bulletin board to motivate students to work hard.

EDUCATION

Purpose: Use this bulletin board to publicize graduation day.

EDUCATION IS PREPARATION

Purpose: Use this bulletin board to motivate students to study hard to prepare for their future.

EDUCATION IS THE SPICE OF LIFE

Purpose: Use this bulletin board to stress the importance of an education.

- -

BE A SENSATION WITH AN EDUCATION

Purpose: This bulletin board will motivate students about the importance of an education.

HEALTH

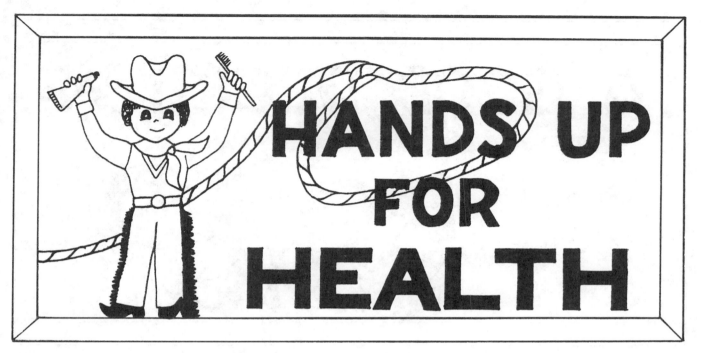

Purpose: This bulletin board will encourage students to be aware of the importance of good dental health habits.

. . . .

DON'T BRUSH OFF DENTAL HEALTH

Purpose: After this bulletin board is displayed, students will be aware of good dental health habits.

HEALTH

Purpose: Use this bulletin board to stress the importance of caring for your vision.

- -

Purpose: This bulletin board will stress the importance of health habits.

HEALTH

CONSIDER YOURSELF
WEALTHY,
IF YOU'RE
HEALTHY

Purpose: Use this bulletin board to promote an awareness of good health habits.

FOR PRECISION

YOU NEED GOOD VISION

Purpose: Use this bulletin board to stress caring for your vision.

Purpose: Use this bulletin board to call attention to the subject of health.

Purpose: Use this bulletin board to encourage good dental health habits.

DON'T LET THE PILGRIMS GET YOU DOWN

Purpose: This bulletin board will announce that Thanksgiving is on its way.

PLEASE BE MINE... MY VALENTINE

Purpose: Use this bulletin board during February for promoting excitement about Valentine's Day.

HO, HO, HO, A MERRY CHRISTMAS **AND AWAY WE GO!**

Purpose: This bulletin board will announce Christmas is on its way.

HANUKAH KEEPS ME SPINNING

Purpose: This bulletin board will announce it's time for Hanukah.

Purpose: Use this bulletin board to announce Halloween is coming.

Purpose: Use this bulletin board in October to call attention to Halloween.

LANGUAGE

Purpose: After this bulletin board has been displayed, students will be able to form the plurals of the words shown. Add new words daily.

Purpose: This bulletin board will introduce synonyms. Have students list synonyms for the words on the clouds. Add new words daily.

LANGUAGE

PLEASE PASS THE PUNCTUATION

Purpose: This bulletin board will illustrate the symbols of punctuation.

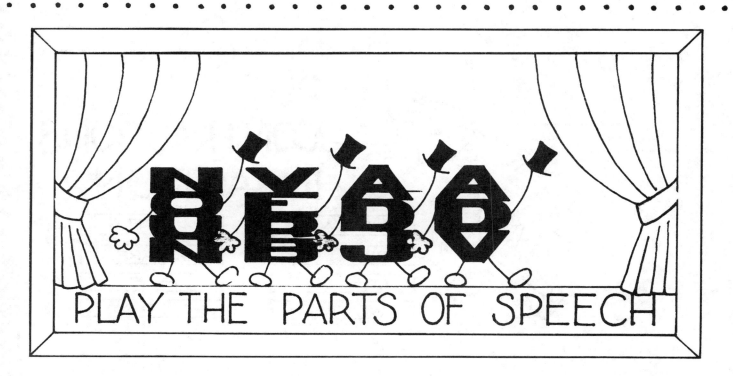

PLAY THE PARTS OF SPEECH

Purpose: After this bulletin board has been displayed, students will be introduced to the parts of speech.

JUMP WORK PLAY RUN SKIP

VERB'S THE WORD

Purpose: This bulletin board will emphasize that a verb is a word showing action.

PUT CONTRACTIONS IN ACTION

THEY WILL	COULD HAVE
WOULD NOT	WE ARE
CAN NOT	HE IS
WE HAVE	SHOULD NOT

Purpose: This bulletin board will introduce the use of contractions by encouraging students to make the contraction.

Purpose: Use this bulletin board to motivate students to read a variety of books.

Purpose: Use this bulletin board to encourage students to visit the library.

LIBRARY

Purpose: Use this bulletin board to encourage students to use the library.

· ·

Purpose: This bulletin board will help motivate students to visit the library and read more books.

JOIN THE LIBRARY LINEUP

Purpose: Use this bulletin board to promote the use of the library.

· ·

THE LIBRARY WILL LIFT YOUR SPIRITS

Purpose: Use this bulletin board during National Book Week to promote the library.

MAGNIFY YOUR MANNERS

Purpose: This bulletin board will be effective in introducing the subject of good manners.

- -

MANNERS
MAKE YOU A WINNER

Purpose: After this bulletin board has been displayed, students will be encouraged to have good manners.

30

MANNERS

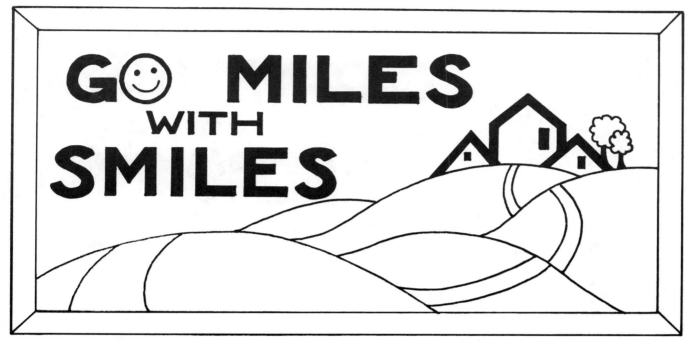

Purpose: Use this bulletin board to encourage students to be kind and friendly.

Purpose: Use this bulletin board to encourage good manners.

MANNERS

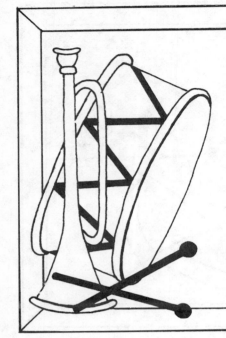

STRIKE UP THE BAND
FOR A HELPING HAND

Purpose: Use this bulletin board to encourage students to help fellow classmates.

MANNERS ARE A *Heavenly* IDEA

Purpose: Use this bulletin board to motivate students to display good manners.

MATH

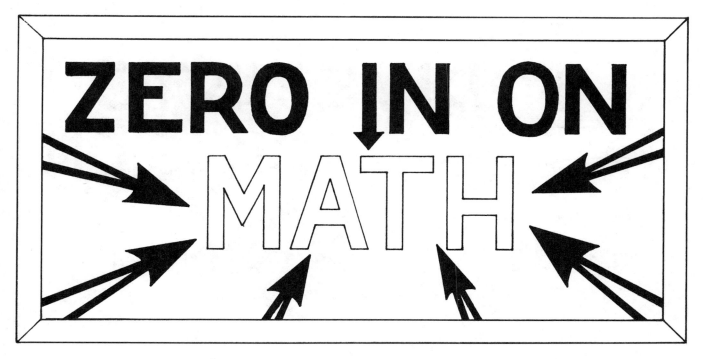

Purpose: Use this bulletin board to interest students in math.

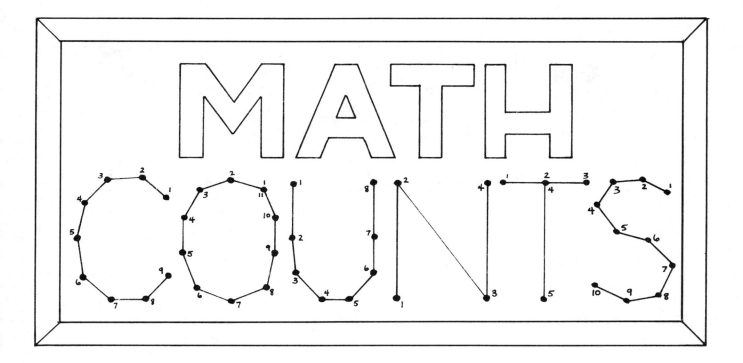

Purpose: Use this bulletin board to promote an interest and excitement for the subject of math.

MATH

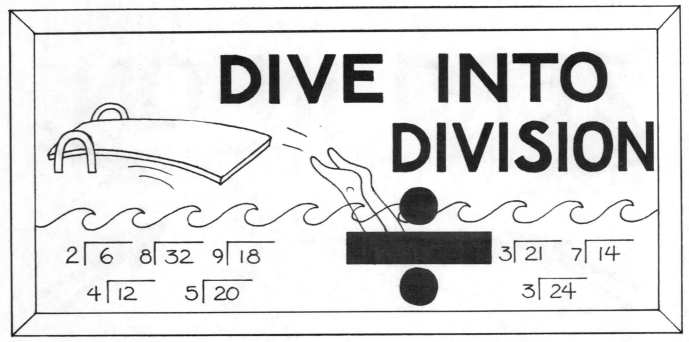

Purpose: After working with this bulletin board, students should be able to divide eight problems correctly in one minute or less.

· ·

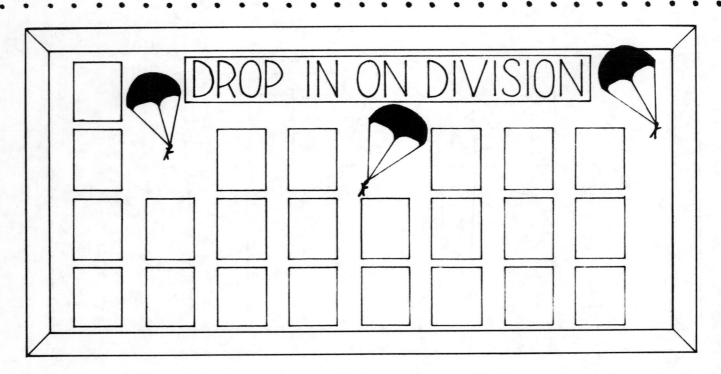

Purpose: Use this bulletin board to display student work on the subject of division.

MATH

TIME OUT FOR MULTIPLICATION

Purpose: Use this bulletin board to display students' work on multiplication.

YOU CAN COUNT ON METRICS

METER   CENTIMETER

LITER   MILLIMETER

CENTILITER   GRAM

Purpose: Use this bulletin board to introduce the metric system.

MATH

GET SCRATCHIN' FOR SUBTRACTION

Purpose: Use this bulletin board to display students' work in subtraction.

- -

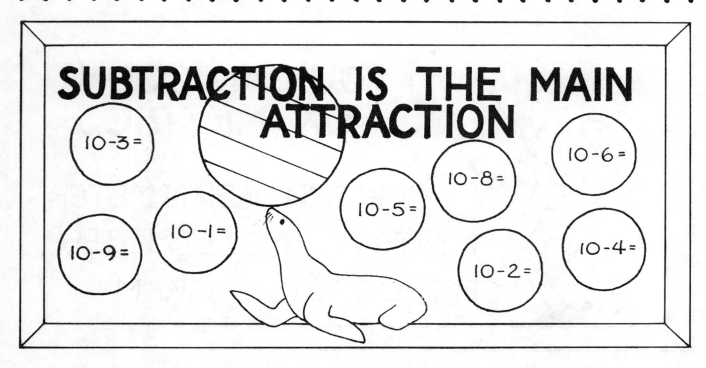

SUBTRACTION IS THE MAIN ATTRACTION

10-3 =
10-6 =
10-8 =
10-5 =
10-1 =
10-9 =
10-4 =
10-2 =

Purpose: After working with this bulletin board, students will be able to subtract eight problems correctly in one minute or less. Add new problems daily.

MATH

Purpose: Use this bulletin board to announce the subject of addition.

Purpose: Use this bulletin board as a learning center for students to practice addition.

MATH

Purpose: This bulletin board should be used to interest students in fractions.

Purpose: After working with this bulletin board, students should be able to add eight fractions in one minute or less.

MUSIC

Purpose: Use this bulletin board to invite students into the wonderful world of music.

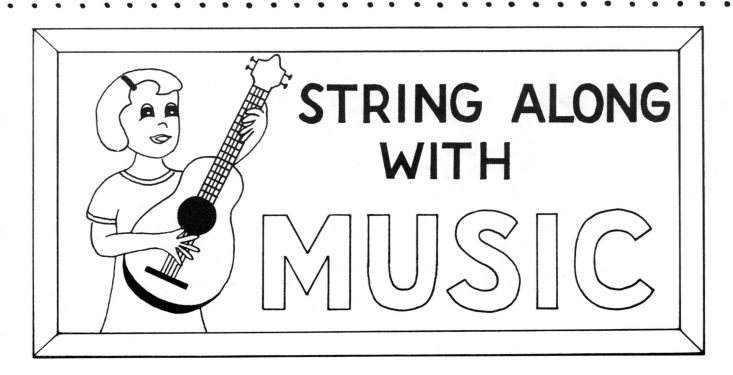

Purpose: Use this bulletin board to introduce students to the variety of string instruments used in music.

Purpose: Use this bulletin board to promote an interest in music.

Purpose: Use this bulletin board to excite students about music.

Purpose: Use this bulletin board to promote excitement for music.

Purpose: Use this bulletin board to promote enthusiasm for music.

NEATNESS

Purpose: Use this bulletin board to encourage neat work.

Purpose: Use this bulletin board to encourage students' work to exhibit neatness.

NEATNESS

Purpose: Use this bulletin board to motivate and praise students for being neat.

Purpose: Use ths board to display students' work exhibiting neatness.

Purpose: Use this bulletin board to help stop littering.

Purpose: Use this bulletin board to encourage students not to litter.

Purpose: Use this bulletin board to encourage students to be neat.

Purpose: Use this bulletin board to stimulate neatness in students' work.

NEWS

Purpose: Use this bulletin board to stress the importance of the news.

Purpose: Use this bulletin board to encourage students' interest in the news.

NEWS

Purpose: Use this bulletin board to increase students' knowledge of identifying captions.

Purpose: Use this bulletin board to interest students in reading the news.

NEWS

NEWS TO CROW ABOUT

Purpose: This bulletin board will display current events.

NEWS TO NIBBLE ON

Purpose: This bulletin board will display current events.

NUTRITION

Purpose: Use this bulletin board to reinforce the four basic food groups for a healthy diet.

Purpose: Use this bulletin board to identify the four basic food groups for a balanced diet.

NUTRITION

Purpose: This bulletin board will stress the importance of good nutrition.

- -

Purpose: Use this bulletin board to encourage students to have good nutrition habits.

MAKE YOUR
MISSION
GOOD
NUTRITION

Purpose: Use this bulletin board to promote good nutrition.

BATTER UP
FOR GOOD
NUTRITION

Purpose: This bulletin board will call attention to good nutrition.

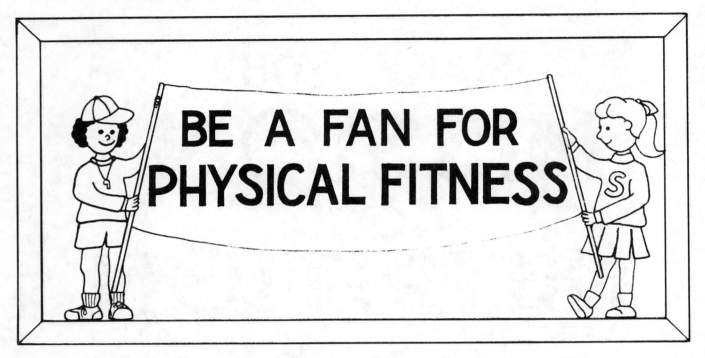

Purpose: This bulletin board will excite students about physical fitness.

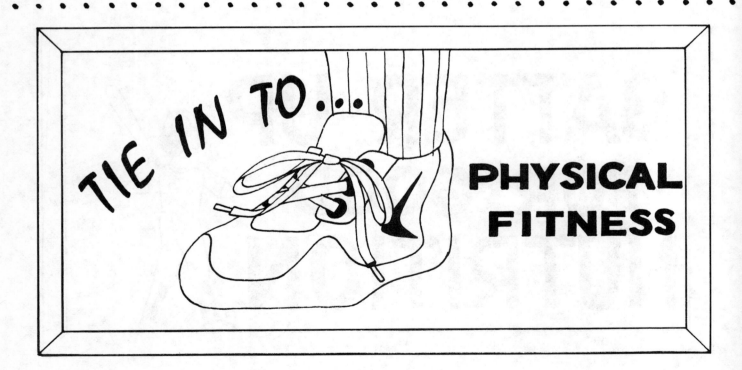

Purpose: Use this bulletin board to encourage students' involvement in physical education.

Purpose: Use this bulletin board to encourage students to be good sports.

Purpose: This bulletin board will encourage students to try physical fitness.

Purpose: This bulletin board will help promote physical fitness.

Purpose: Use this bulletin board to interest students in physical fitness.

Purpose: Use this bulletin board to promote physical fitness.

Purpose: This bulletin board will motivate students to be interested in physical fitness.

Purpose: Use this bulletin board to make students aware of the fun they will have in physical education.

HAVE FUN WITH FITNESS

Purpose: Use this bulletin board to promote physical fitness.

READING

YOU DESERVE A **BOOK** TODAY

Purpose: Use this bulletin board to stimulate students to get involved in reading.

GET IN THE RING WITH READING

Purpose: Use this bulletin board to encourage students to read.

READING

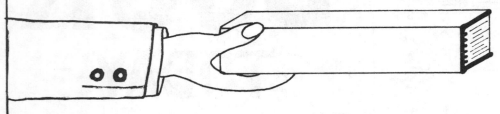

PUT YOUR BEST BOOK
FORWARD

Purpose: Use this bulletin board to encourage students to read
five new books.

· ·

GET A

BOOM
OUT OF
BOOKS

Purpose: Use this bulletin board to excite students about reading
books.

READING

Purpose: After this bulletin board has been displayed, students will be encouraged to read.

Purpose: Use this bulletin board to promote an awareness of the importance of reading to learn.

READING

Purpose: Use this bulletin board to promote excitement for reading.

Purpose: Use this bulletin board to encourage students to read.

Purpose: Use this bulletin board to motivate students to read books on their favorite hobbies.

Purpose: Use this bulletin board to show the value of reading.

SAFETY

Purpose: Use this bulletin board to help promote safety.

Purpose: This bulletin board will call attention to safety.

Purpose: Use this bulletin board to help promote safety.

Purpose: Use this bulletin board to help promote safety.

Purpose: This bulletin board will help call attention to safety.

Purpose: Use this bulletin board to highlight safety.

Purpose: Use this bulletin board to announce the month of September and back to school.

Purpose: Display this bulletin board in September to welcome students to school.

Purpose: This bulletin board should be used to announce the coming of the change of seasons.

Purpose: Use this bulletin board to promote excitement for fall.

SEASONAL

FOCUS IN ON FALL

Purpose: This bulletin board should be used to highlight fall events.

FLIP OVER FALL

Purpose: This bulletin board will promote enthusiasm for fall.

Purpose: Use this bulletin board to display your students' names for open house at PTA.

Purpose: Use this bulletin board to promote excitement for the month of November.

SEASONAL

DELIGHTED
OVER
DECEMBER

Purpose: Use this bulletin board to promote excitement for
December.

JOIN THE JUMP
~for~
JANUARY

DISPLAY WORK HERE

Purpose: Use this bulletin board to display students' New Year's
resolutions.

Purpose: Use this bulletin board to promote excitement over the coming of winter.

Purpose: Use this bulletin board to encourage students to study.

Purpose: Use this bulletin board to promote good feelings about February.

Purpose: Use this bulletin board to encourage enthusiasm for February.

SEASONAL

WE HIGHLIGHT THESE HEROES

- JESSE OWENS
- MARTIN LUTHER
- GEORGE WASHINGTON CARVER
- BOOKER T. WASHINGTON

Purpose: Use this bulletin board to recognize these outstanding Black Americans. Display this board during Black History Week.

READY OR NOT

HERE I COME

Purpose: Use this bulletin board in February to announce Groundhog Day.

SEASONAL

Purpose: Use this bulletin board in March to reinforce students'
skills in measuring.

Purpose: Use this bulletin board to encourage good listening
habits in April.

Purpose: Use this bulletin board to call attention to spring.

Purpose: Use this bulletin board to encourage students to study in spring.

Purpose: Use this bulletin board to call attention to May events.

Purpose: Use this bulletin board to display students' work in any subject during the month of May.

Purpose: This bulletin board will get students excited about the coming of summer.

Purpose: This bulletin board will announce the coming of summer.

Purpose: Use this bulletin board to promote students' building their self-confidence.

Purpose: Use this bulletin board to encourage good habits for a good self-concept.

SCIENCE

Purpose: Use this bulletin board to encourage students to work hard in science.

Purpose: Use this bulletin board to highlight subjects studied in science.

Purpose: Use this bulletin board to promote excitement for the subject of science.

Purpose: Use this bulletin board to get students interested in the subject of science.

THE WORLD MAKES "SCENTS" WITH SCIENCE

Purpose: Use this bulletin board to call attention to the subject of science.

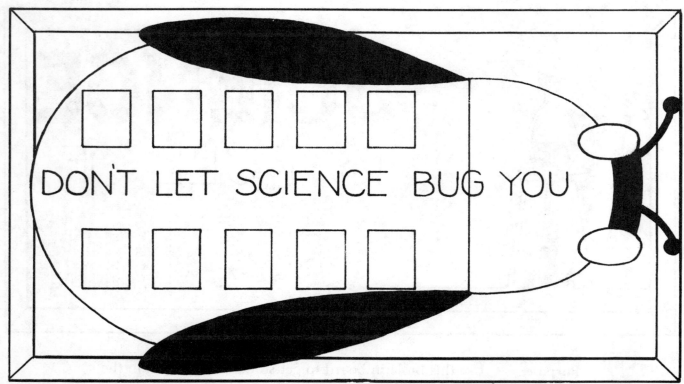

DON'T LET SCIENCE BUG YOU

Purpose: Use this bulletin board when studying bugs, insects, etc., in science. Have an art activity and let students create bugs. Display work on bulletin board.

SCIENCE

SCIENCE WILL SEND YOU

Purpose: Use this bulletin board when studying space in science.
Have a paper airplane contest.

SCIENCE IS ELECTRIFYING

Purpose: Use this bulletin board when studying electricity in science.

Purpose: Use this bulletin board to introduce the use and purpose of a microscope.

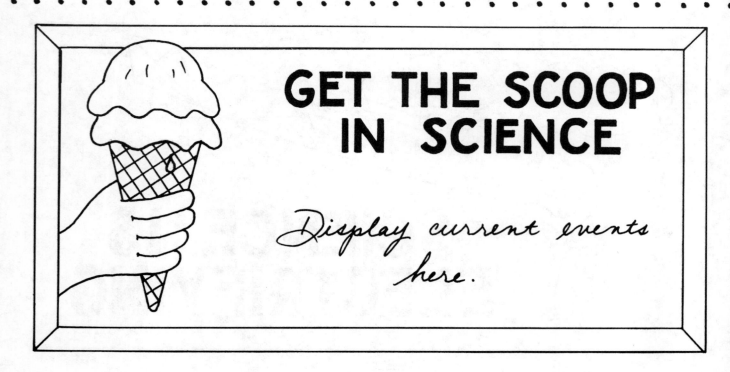

Purpose: Use this bulletin board to display current events in science.

SOCIAL STUDIES

Purpose: After this bulletin board has been displayed, students will be able to name the capitals of the states displayed. Add new states each day.

Purpose: Use this bulletin board to promote an interest in social studies.

Purpose: Use this bulletin board to call attention to social studies.

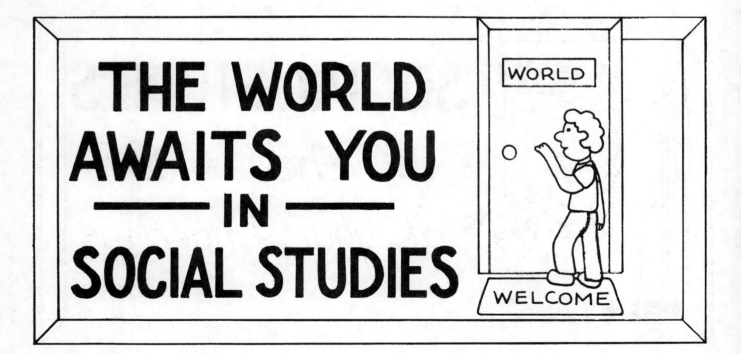

Purpose: Use this bulletin board to promote excitement for the subject of social studies.

SOCIAL STUDIES IS A SNAP

Purpose: Use this bulletin board to promote an interest in the subject of social studies.

SIGNS POINT TO SOCIAL STUDIES

Purpose: Use this bulletin board to announce the subject of social studies and to call attention to it.

✓ SPELLING

Purpose: Use this bulletin board to encourage correct spelling.

Purpose: After this bulletin board has been displayed, students will be able to spell new words you select. Write spelling words on the bones.

SPELLING

Purpose: Use this bulletin board to call attention to the subject of spelling.

Purpose: After this bulletin board has been displayed, students will increase their spelling vocabulary. Play a game by having one student pitch verbally a new word and another student batter up and try to spell it correctly.

SPELLING

Purpose: Use this bulletin board to encourage correct spelling.

Purpose: Use this bulletin board to encourage correct spelling.

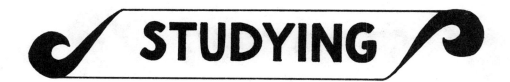

HEADS UP FOR HOMEWORK

Purpose: Use this bulletin board to encourage students to study and to do their homework.

GET A HOLD ON HOMEWORK

Purpose: Use this bulletin board to encourage students to study and to do their homework.

STUDYING

Purpose: Use this bulletin board to encourage students to study.

Purpose: Use this bulletin board to encourage students to study and to do their homework.